Contents

Introduction

"You can lead a toddler to the potty, but you can't make him pee."
Unknown

I want to thank you and congratulate you for downloading the book, " *Potty Training In 3 Days: Quick and Easy Guide to Potty Training Your Toddler In As Short As 3 days* " .

Potty Training isn't the easiest thing in the world. It can truly put your patience to the test.

This book contains proven steps and strategies on how to potty train your child from the signs that say he's ready to be potty-trained, to what you should do, how to make sure your strategies work, potty training myths, and more.

I am a mother of three, and I remember not having a notion of where to start with this. I felt silly even asking someone as I felt like it was something that was obvious to most people and as a mother it was something I should instinctually know.

Because of my lack of knowledge, I struggled with my first child. When the time got close to training my second child, I decided I wanted to be a lot more prepared. I read every book I could find on the topic and this time I would not be caught off guard. When I did this I noticed some problems with the books I was reading. I found a lot of the information and methods given seemed too forceful and traumatizing to the child. I also found that a lot of the books where very long and stretched out the process to fill the pages of their book.

I did take a little something from every book I read and started to implement it. I began working as a child minder then and learned through a process of trial and error and began to hone my skills over the years. I optimized the process as best as I could to the stage where it usually took me about 3 days to potty train a new child.

I wrote this book to share some insight and basics on this process. It is intentionally short as when you have a toddler, time is a luxury you often don't have. I have also given a method that I believe is the least traumatic for the child and I one that I believe will significantly help you on this journey.

Thanks again for getting the book, I hope you enjoy it.

Chapter 1: Signs that Your Child Is Ready for Potty Training

First things first, you have to check if your child is ready to be potty-trained or not. If a child is not ready, no matter what you do, you won't be able to train them.

Here's some indicators to keep in mind:

1) Is the child already able to stay dry for at least 2 hours or longer during the day?

2) Does your child already know how to follow basic directions or do they know how to copy you when you tell them to do so?

3) Is your child eager to please, and do they have a desire to be praised?

4) Do they now seem interested in the potty chair, toilet or the bathroom?

5) Do they now seem interested in wearing underwear?

6) Do they now complain about diapers that are dry or wet? Do they know the differences between the two?

7) Can they run and walk now?

8) Do they like things to be in their proper places?

9) Do they now try to dress themselves?

10) Do they now tell you that they want to pee or poop through facial expressions or words?

11) Is your child now able to sit, and then rise from a potty chair?

12) Do they know how to pull their pants down, and put them up again?

13) Are they familiar with potty lingo, such as *wet, dry, pee, poop, bowl, bottom, clean,* or *messy/dirty*?

If your answer to a lot of these is "yes", then chances are, your child is ready to be potty-trained. If they are, proceed to the next chapter so can learn where to start.

Chapter 2: What You Need to Do

Now that your child is ready to be potty-trained, let us talk about how to do it.

Start with a Positive Attitude

More than anything, you need to have a positive attitude. This will show your child that the activity is fun, and it's not something they should be scared of. When the activity becomes fun and exciting the process will be substantially smoother.

Prepare the Equipment…and Use a Doll!

Put the potty chair in the bathroom. It can also be helpful if you let the child decorate the equipment to help to increase their positive associations with this process.

Another trick that can lighten the mood of this journey is using a doll throughout the process. You can first show them how to use the equipment by making use of a doll. You see, dolls often make kids feel like they are not alone. When you use a doll as a way to teach a child what they should do, they can relate a lot easier.

For example, bring the doll to the potty chair and let it sit down. Make potty noises, and then help the doll down, and say "good job" You could even give the doll a "star", or any form of praise. When the child sees this, they'll realize that *"this is what I should do."* They will also know that it's okay and that it should be done on the potty chair. It will clearly show to them that this is something good that is to be praised.

Where to begin

When starting off, it's best to choose an entire day when you are completely free. I know this can be difficult for some parents, but I urge you to find the time. If you do this it will speed up the learning curve of the child and make the process easier. During this day your child will need your undivided attention, so try your best to make sure everything is taken care of.

Tell your child something along the lines of "Today we are going to learn to go potty like a big boy." Say this as if it's something very exciting that the child will enjoy. "This will be fun," will be the frame for the entire process.

For the entire first day your child will be naked or bottomless. This is because throughout this day you are going to try to catch your child when they are peeing. You will then get them to the potty as they are peeing. Makes sure the potty is close by at all times and try to move fast when you are getting them to the potty. It can be frightening for the child if you move too quickly so judge an acceptable speed.

When the child starts peeing, try not to overreact. Simply tell your child in a calm tone to "Hold it in," and put them on the potty immediately. For boys, when they are on the potty, hold their penis down and teach him to do this himself. Once they have gone, try and reinforce this new behavior with a reward of praise. You can say something along the lines of "Wow, well done." We are trying to implement a sense of achievement for the child every time they go.

To help to encourage this peeing process it also helps to keep your child hydrated throughout this day. You should aim for slightly more fluid than usual, but, don't overdo it.

I must stress it is important that you keep a strong focus on your child throughout the day as you will want to catch them peeing as soon as you can. To pass the time I recommend playing games with them, reading books and performing other pass times. It is a stressful time for both of you, and it helps to get some quality time with them.

During the day, you might notice your child give a funny look or behaving in a certain way before they pee. As the training continues throughout the day, you will notice your child start to realize their need to pee earlier and earlier. They are starting to make a connection in their brains between the feeling and the action of going to the potty.

A lot of methods start off with you placing your child on the potty multiple times a day. However, I believe my way, at least for the first day, is more effective. I believe it helps the child associate the potty with peeing and pooping much better.

Teaching the child to poop

When your child is trying to poop you should notice a concentrated look, grunting or another sign of discomfort. When this happens, simply sit the child on the potty and encourage them, tell them that they can do it. Try your best to avoid being forceful or commanding as this may make it more difficult. It is best to give gentle encouragement and guidance. If your child starts crying, just try to be supportive and try your best to comfort them.

Praise your child if they are successful and let them know that they have done well. If your child doesn't poop or you miss them pooping on the first day, make sure to tell them "Poop goes in the potty," in a stern enough tone that they will get the message. However, once again it is best to not be overly critical of them as this is a hard and tiresome day for you both.

Napping

During this first day, it is important to use diapers for naps and at night time. Naps are also important for keeping your child in a mood in which they will be willing to learn. It becomes extremely difficult to teach a cranky child.

Day 2

On day two we are going to schedule potty breaks throughout the day, and we are still ready to deal with them if they happen outside of these scheduled times. On this day we are going to have the child wearing clothes. Something to note here is to make sure the pants are easy to get off. I also suggest starting the child with going commando for at least the next week. I believe the child is a lot more likely to catch themselves peeing much faster this way. This is because it is a lot more of an uncomfortable feeling for them and is a significantly different feeling than wearing diapers.

Now schedule times throughout the day for them to go to the potty. This should be preferably after meals when they are more likely to go. You may already know a time when your child regularly does their business. If this is the case; then take them to the potty and take their diaper off at this time.

Your child's new found interest in the potty may begin to waver at this stage as they get more accustomed to it. It is important to keep your child amused at this stage, so make sure you bring a toy or a book to the potty with them.

When you are just starting off, don't worry if they haven't pooped at the end of your scheduled session. Simply put their diaper back on. This is a very different environment for them to poop and can take some time for them to get used to it. Just carry on as usual until the next scheduled practice.

Day 3

Once day 3 comes along it can be easy to get frustrated if your child is progressing slower than you had hoped. You must remember every child is different and putting pressure on them will only inhibit their learning. Every child learns at different rates We must keep our patience.

On day 3 and beyond we are going to continue as before with our scheduled times throughout the day. Now we will try to promote our child to tell you if they need to go. Do this by emphasizing how well they are doing when they do manage to tell you. We are rewarding them with praise to help them to create the connections they need in their brains. If this doesn't happen immediately don't worry your child will eventually get to the stage of telling you.

How to deal with NO.

Eventually, you may be met with a strong "no" when you ask your toddler to go to the potty. It is important that you do not make this a battle of wills. This will be counterproductive, instead, respect their decision. Do not get upset if they then have an accident, simply reinforce that they should go to the potty to pee. If they do this it is also important you do not comfort them and tell them it is all right. If you do this after they have had an accident this could reinforce the behavior as your toddler doesn't understand the subtleties of language yet.

Resistance will come eventually so expect it and plan for it. If you do not make a big deal out of it, their resistance should be short lived.

Teach the child how to clean

A big part of potty training a child is helping them learn how to clean up too, especially with girls.

What you have to do is tell her that she should carefully wipe herself from the front all the way to the back so that germs would not fester her body. Teach her so she will know what's hygienic and what isn't.

Once they know how to clean themselves then teach the child how to flush their business. Show them how it's done on the toilet. Once they learn how to do it, they'll be more responsible when it comes to cleaning up. Of course, do not forget to tell the child to wash his or her hands afterward. Again, proper hygiene is very important.

Some Rewards and Incentives During Training

Give them a book or a toy

It will also be quite helpful if you give your child a toy or a potty-training related book for kids (*Once Upon a Potty, I Want My Potty, Sam's Potty*) so that potty training will be a fun and engaging learning experience for him.

At first, you do have to stay with your child while they're at their potty place, just to make sure that they're using the potty seat properly, and that they're not uncomfortable. Eventually, they'll learn to tell you to stay away, and that they know what needs to be done already. For the start, however, it's important that you stay with them at first for proper support.

If you go on vacation, it is important to bring the potty seat or check if the place has a child-friendly toilet seat, so you can continue practicing. It is important to be consistent at this phase in your child's life.

Other Incentives

Here's a list of other incentives that you can use:

1. **Coloring Books**. Help the child become more artistic by letting them work on a coloring book after each potty training session. Let them choose the book they want to use so that they will be interested.

2. **Buy a Drink-and-Wet Doll!** You may think it's icky, but what better way to teach a child how to potty—and buy her a new toy, too—than by using a doll, specifically the *Drink-and-Wet Doll*! What this doll does is that you get to feed it or let it drink, and then she pees after. Bring her to the potty seat and your child will surely realize what needs to be done and have fun at it, too.

3. **Help them Decorate a Door Hanger**. Color it, add stickers, let them write, etc. What matters is that they'll have something to hang on the door when they feel like they have to go potty. Once they have something like this, they will be more than willing to potty because they'll be excited to use what they had made earlier.

4. **Make a Lollipop Tree.** This is just a makeshift tree made from lollipops. Give one to your child after each potty session and chances are, they will look forward to those sessions more.

5. **Make a Happy Jar.** On popsicle sticks, write about fun things you can do in a day, or maybe during the weekend. For example, *see Frozen again, go to a theme park, make pizza*, etc. Put them in a large glass jar and have your kid pick one after each potty session. Surprises often make kids happy, and this one will surely help him learn and be happy at the same time.

6. **A Toy "Vending" Machine**. Buy one of those toy vending machines that have little toys inside them, and let your child get one after each potty session.

7. **Make a level jar**. Put some labels outside the jar. The one on the lowest would be for the first few days of potty training, and the one on top will be the best reward. Let your child add two marbles after each successful potty training session, and they'll be

interested in learning—because they'll realize that in a few weeks' time, they will get something really good.

When you have the right incentives, potty training would be so much better.

Chapter 3: How to Keep Your Potty Training Methods Working

Of course, when you potty train a child, you don't just stop when you feel like they've learned it all. There are certain things you have to do to make sure that the skill becomes internalized.

Think of it this way: suppose you were taught a lesson on a completely new topic today, would it just be embedded in your mind right away? Probably not, you would most certainly have to revise the information a couple of times before it sank in.

So, when it comes to potty training, you have to make sure that you do the following:

Be Patient—Even When the Child Says They Don't Want to Go Potty

Well, maybe he just does not want to go yet. Or maybe, he's shy or doesn't know what to do.

Yes, this can be frustrating, especially because you know you're just trying to do the right thing. But, you might just terrify or traumatize the child if you go and get mad at them because they do not want to go potty.

Take a Laidback Approach

Again, your child will learn better when they feel like potty training is a fun experience and that it's not something they should be scared of. When you become so angry or so strict, chances are, your child will feel like potty training is scary or that they are being reprimanded, that's not the kind of thing you want to foster.

The key here is to realize that a child learns via positive reinforcement and not by being reprimanded.

Clap Your Hands, Laugh—Keep a Lively Atmosphere During Each Session

You have to remember that kids are naturally playful. Even if it takes them a few tries to get there. You have to realize that they're trying and that in itself is already a good thing.

The very second your child gets on the potty seat, go ahead and praise them. This is already an achievement. When the child feels that they're being encouraged early on they become more confident about themselves. Be the kind of parent who's willing to lead and encourage him every step of the way.

What to do when travelling

If you go on vacation, it is important to bring the potty seat or check if the place has a child-friendly toilet seat, so you can continue practicing. It is important to be consistent at this phase in your child's life.

Realize that they might not learn everything RIGHT AWAY

Again, things like this always take time. They don't just happen right off the bat. Remember just because you've taught your child how to be potty-trained today doesn't mean they'll already be an expert tomorrow. They might need to relearn lessons. So it is best to not get upset, and to simply show them the process again if they are confused.

Respect Your Child's Learning Curve

Children have different learning curves. Some learn easily, but others simply don't, but that does not mean they're not perfect or there's something wrong or terrible with them. Albert Einstein didn't speak until he was four years old, people learn at different rates, and we shouldn't judge.

When you start comparing your child to others, you're also beginning to start a painful relationship between you two. Cut it out, be patient, and know that your child will learn eventually. Put yourself in their shoes and learn to be mindful of this phase in his life.

Be Consistent

Consistency is the key to the success of almost everything. If you want to train your child, know that you have to be consistent. Do it on schedule, and chances are, they'll pick it up faster than you think.

Once you keep this in mind, you'll make things easier for both of you.

Make Sure to Go Potty Fast

Now, when you see signs that your child wants to go potty or use the toilet, even if it's not on the schedule, go and bring them to their potty place right away. Take note that if they feel the need to urinate or potty, and it is out of schedule, you don't have to get mad or scold them. In fact, you should go ahead and praise them because they're telling you or showing you that they want to urinate or potty, that is already an improvement on itself, instead of them using diapers all the time.

At night, it would be best to bring them to their potty place before going to sleep so bedwetting could be avoided especially if they're already wearing underpants. If they want to pee at night, tell them to wake you up and please be patient to help them out.

Pulls-Ups or Underwear

This depends on the child, either or, can work however you should address this issue concerning your child's personality and their experience so far with potty training. For example, if certain children are provided with pull ups, they might be inclined to stay and keep playing after accidents happen. Whereas other children have a sense of self-pride when they go to the potty and when they feel an accident coming, they will rush to the potty. I do not recommend letting them wear pull ups during the first couple of weeks of potty training. This is because it will take away some of the child's drive to make it to the potty.

It is also useful to test your child in different environments as they might be potty trained at home, but when you take them somewhere else this could be entirely different. So it's a process of trial and error from this stage. If possible prepare for the worst, I would recommend using pull ups for a little while after your child has been trained, particularly when you leave the house.

If you want to introduce underwear to a child who is potty trained but put off by the inconvenience of going potty, I would recommend switching to underwear. It will become uncomfortable for the child, and they will act out of necessity. You can also add in an extra motivation, by getting special underwear for them, for example, a pair with superheroes on them or their favorite T.V. show character.

Cost is also a factor as pull ups will be more expensive than regular diapers and so are preferably a very temporary solution.

Chapter 4: Signs that a Child Is Already Potty-Trained

So, how exactly would you know that your child is already potty-trained? Here's what you have to be mindful of:

They already know, and they tell you if their underwear is wet

The very sign that a child is already potty-trained or is getting there is if they know they have wet their underwear. This is a sign that they're already hygienic, and they know that they have to go somewhere to pee or poop, and not just in their underwear.

They're eager to get their rewards

Why? Because they know that what they're doing is something good, and they want to prove that they are learning.

When a child learns the ideas of rewards and positive reinforcement, they begin to have that healthy competitive streak in them. This is something good because it shows that they're understanding what you're trying to teach them. They know they will get rewards if they do something good, so of course, they will work on doing that.

They go to the potty chair and try especially when they feel like they want to pee or poop

Another big sign that they're learning is when they go to their chair, and try to go potty. For one, they want to please you, and then they also know that this is right. And when they try to do what's right, it means that they are learning, and you're doing something right.

They're proud of their new underpants

When they want to pick new underpants, it means that they knows they're no longer a baby and because they are no longer a "baby," they will be more responsible about their pee and poop!

Chapter 5: Signs That a Potty-Training Child Needs to See a Doctor

There are also times when your child seems to have an extremely hard time being potty-trained because it's a sign that they probably need to be seen by a doctor.

How do you know if your child has to visit a doctor? Keep these things in mind:

They strain while trying to pee

This is a sign that there is something wrong. Do not wait for it to get worse because even if you can't see anything, there might be something wrong, so take him to the doctor right away.

They Have not Had a Bowel Movement in Three Days

A person, especially a child has to have a bowel movement every day. Otherwise, there might be a blockage in the rectum, and that's not a good thing. It might bring infections, and those are things you don't want your child to be afflicted with. It could simply be because he ate something that's making it hard for him to poop. Either way, medical attention should be sought to make sure.

They're still bedwetting, and they're already 5 years old

This is a problem that some parents encounter with their kids. In fact, around 90% of kids wet the bed, but the problem gets worse if the child is already 5 years and above.

Sometimes, bedwetting is inherited. But other times, certain issues make bedwetting happen, and some of these are as follows:

1. **Deep Sleeping.** Some kids are deep sleepers and struggle to wake up to pee.
2. **Low Anti-Diuretic Hormone.** When a child is afflicted with this,

his hormones automatically tell his kidneys that he should not urinate so much, or that the kidneys should not make a lot of urine. And thus, what happens is that the kid releases the hormones when he is asleep—and thus, bedwetting happens.

3. **Delayed Bladder Maturation.** Some kids' bladders do not mature as fast as others.—and their bladder fails to communicate with their brains while they're asleep.

4. **Constipation.** Sometimes, a kid wets the bed because he's constipated.

5. **Small "Functional" Bladder.** Sometimes, a kid's bladder sends signals to the brain that it's already full—even when it's not—and so, bedwetting happens.

They have frequent stains on their underwear

These might be poop that got out when it wasn't time.. Sometimes, it's not just bowel stains you have to be mindful of but also bleeding or signs of wounds or laceration. Do not hesitate to take him to the doctor right away.

They know how to use the potty, but still have wet pants now and then

This happens. Sometimes, a child is already trained, but there are moments when he'd get too wet his pants maybe because he has bedwetting or embarrassment issues, and these have to be talked about before they get worse.

He only pees every 8 to 9 hours

Even for an adult, this is not healthy. A normal person should pee every 3 to 4 hours. Otherwise, the bladder might suffer, especially if the person has a naturally small bladder.

When a child does not pee as much as he should, it can lead to problems with his kidneys. So, make sure you have him checked right away.

Their Pee Hurts or Burns or They Have Intermittent Pee Stream

These are signs that a person has Urinary Tract Infection, and that's not an easy thing to deal with. Sometimes, it causes the genitals to blow up, or the kid to suffer from rashes, and of course, embarrassment, at some point.

They Complain of Hurtful Bowel Movements

There are times when they may or could suffer from bowel movements that are extremely hurtful because the bowel can't get out of the rectum easily, or because there are irritations and bleeding involved.

Remember that some kids can't easily speak up about what they're feeling— and it's your job as a parent or a guardian to make them feel like they can talk to you. Don't let things take a turn for the worse, and take them to be seen by a doctor—stat.

Chapter 6: Potty Training Myths — Debunked!

Finally, here are some common Potty Training Myths—all debunked for you!

"If I put my baby on the potty seat when he's 1 to 1 ½ years old, he'll easily know what's up!"

Your child will probably have no idea what the potty is to start off with, never mind how to use it.

What you can do here is guide him. Help him understand what the potty seat is about. Follow the tips that were mentioned earlier. Be the guiding force that your child needs you to be.

Do not expect your child to understand what something is about when you have not shown them yet. Everything starts with you.

"Your child's life will be ruined if you mess up his schedule for potty training."

No. You're not going to ruin your child's life just because you have messed up his potty training schedule, or allowed him to go potty when it's past his bedtime.

Potty training, as much as it is for your child, is a good training for you, too. It teaches you to be patient. It also helps you to believe in what your child CAN do, instead of what he CANNOT do. Potty training is different for everyone, and you won't mess up your child's life if you makes mistakes. Learn from the experience, and don't treat it as something terrible.

"It will just lead to arguments between my child and me."

Never think of potty training this way. Instead, think of it as a way to help you and your child bond— crucial for his growing years. Think of it as a way to show your child that you care. It is also a time where you can spend quality time with them. Hold the thought that you're helping your child grow into the best person he can be.

Just like anything else in life, when you focus on the positive part of potty training, you will realize how amazing it is. You will always remember this time during their life and though it may be stressful now, you'll cherish these memories later in life.

Printed in Great Britain
by Amazon